Read and Write Chinese

Semmi M. C. Brown

Greenwood Press

GREENWOOD PRESS
47 Pokfulam Road, Basement, Hong Kong.
Telephone: 2546 8212

First published 1994

Reprinted 1996, 2002.

ISBN 962-279-147-6

PRINTED IN HONG KONG BY
NGAI SHING PRINTING CO.

Contents

Unit	Radicals	Examples	
1 人 (human)	亻, 人	你 (you)	14
2 刀 (knife)	刀, 刂	分, 利 (divide, sharp)	19
3 口 (mouth)	口	吃 (eat)	24
4 土 (land)	土, 圡	地, 坐 (floor, sit)	29
5 大 (big)	大	太 (too)	34
6 小 (small)	小	少 (less)	39
7 女 (female)	女	她 (she)	44
8 子 (son)	孑, 子	孩, 孕 (child, pregnant)	49
9 心 (heart)	心, 忄	想 (think)	54
10 手 (hand)	扌	打 (hit)	59
11 日 (sun)	曰, 日	早 (morning)	64
12 月 (moon)	月, 月	朋 (friend)	69

Introduction

The aim of this book is to give foreign learners the ability to understand, read and write Chinese in a systematic way.

In common written Chinese, there are roughly 200 commonly used character fragments or *radicals* 部首 (boh sáu / bou⁶ sau² / bù shǒu). Chinese characters are often composed of many fragments, and it is frequently possible to determine the approximate meaning of a character by examining the component pieces to determine the primary radical in the character.

For example, when the learners have learnt the radical for "mouth" (口), they will know that characters utilising this radical have some relationship with the mouth: 吃 is to eat, 唱 is to sing, and so on.

Armed with this knowledge, the learners will be able to infer the correct meaning of many of the Chinese characters they encounter, even if they are unfamiliar with the complete definition of the character.

This book introduces twenty of the most easily recognisable radicals.

Each unit in the book introduces a new radical and presents an example sentence with characters containing this radical. A series of related characters are then introduced with two commonly used Cantonese pronunciation systems: Yale and Lau, as well as Pinyin, the standard Putonghua pronunciation system. Each unit continues with guided writing practices and finishes with a number of activity-based exercises to reinforce learning and test understanding. The last unit provides review exercises.

Each unit also shows an ancient form of the radical. Although these are no longer used in common writing, they are often employed for decorative purposes.

In this book, the presentation of each radical follows Chinese dictionary order: radicals with fewest strokes are introduced first.

Two written types of Chinese characters are adopted in this book to help learners familiarise themselves with different Chinese writing forms. The first is "Kai Shu" 楷書 which is the standard writing script form and the basis of the printed form used today. The second is "Sung Style" 宋體 which has been largely adopted by Hong Kong newspapers.

One particular problem for Cantonese learners is that the way Cantonese speakers speak is different from the way they write.

For example: "We go swimming."
Cantonese speakers say: 我地去游水。

(Ngóh dei heui yàuh séui)

(Ngoh[5] dei[6] hui[3] yau[4] sui[2].)

But they write: 我們去游泳。

(Ngóh mùhn heui yàuh wihng.)

(Ngoh[5] moon[4] hui[3] yau[4] wing[6].)

Putonghua speakers write and speak the same: 我們去游泳。

(Wǒ men qù yóu yǒng.)

The writing structure of Cantonese is very similar to that of Putonghua though the pronunciation systems are different.

This book introduces the written form of Chinese, and also supplies Cantonese and Putonghua pronunciations.

It is hoped that this book will give learners a systematic introduction to the complexities of Chinese characters and an easy understanding of their structure and meaning.

Introduction to Chinese Writing

Chinese characters have been developed and used for more than two thousand years when the scholar, Hui San, invented six ways of creating Chinese words. Four were used to explain the creation of characters and two described their usage. The four primary methods are as follows:

1. 象形 (jeuhng yìhng / jeung⁶ ying⁴) (xiàng xíng)*

    "Image shapes", or so called "picture characters." The characters describe real objects making words such as sun and moon:

    ⊙ = 日   月 =月

2. 指事 (jí sih / ji² si⁶) (zhǐ shì)

    "Pointing to matters", "indirect symbols" or "ideographs." The examples shown below were orginally formed by adding a dot above or below a horizontal line meaning up (above) or down (below).

    • = 上   = 下

3. 形聲 (yìhng sìng / ying⁴ sing¹) (xíng shēng)

    "Determinative-phonetic characters." The combination of a radical suggesting the sense of the word plus a phonetic part indicating the pronunciation of the word. For example: river is written with the radical of three drops of water, indicating river is related to water, but it is pronounced as "hòh/hoh⁴" "hé" because the phonetic "hó/hoh²" "kě" is attached to it:

氵	+	可	=	河
water	+	hó / hoh² kě	=	hòh / hoh⁴ (river) hé
扌	+	足	=	捉
hand	+	jùk / juk¹ zú	=	jùk /juk¹ (catch) zhuō

---

* Pronunciation guides are given in the order: (Yale / Lau) (Pinyin). See pages 9–13 for more details.

4. 會意 (wuih yi / wui⁶ yi³) (huì yì)

"Meeting of ideas" or "associative compound." Two or more pictographs or ideographs are combined to form a new character to indicate a new idea. For example: "good" is made up of a girl and a boy. It must be good to have both a daughter and a son in a family:

女 + 子 = 好   (daughter + son = good)
日 + 月 = 明   (sun + moon = bright)

There are altogether over 60,000 different Chinese characters and about 3,000 are commonly used. It sounds difficult to learn them all but it is not as difficult as it looks once you have mastered the rules and the structural framework.

Chinese characters are comprised of many strokes, each stroke has its own unique order in writing. This is called "pen order." One stroke is defined as the path from the point you put down your pen till you pick up your pen. For example, 丁 and 乙 is one stroke because you have to write it altogether without breaking it up. Examples of two-stroke characters are 人，刀 and those require three-stroke characters include 大，口，子. Some words are more complicated and contain more strokes such as 鸚 (parrot) has 28 strokes and 籲 (exhort) has 32.

There are eight basic strokes in Chinese writing:

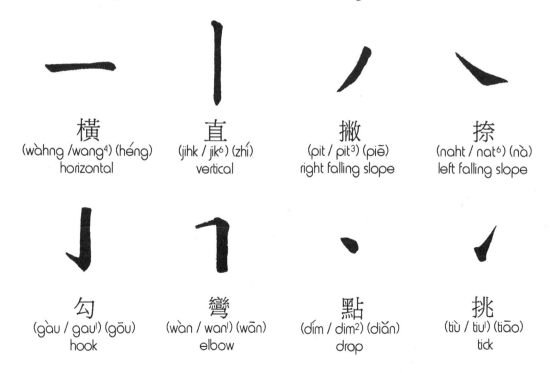

橫
(wàhng /wang⁴) (héng)
horizontal

直
(jihk / jik⁶) (zhí)
vertical

撇
(pit / pit³) (piē)
right falling slope

捺
(naht / nat⁶) (nà)
left falling slope

勾
(gàu / gau¹) (gōu)
hook

彎
(wàn / wan¹) (wān)
elbow

點
(dím / dim²) (diǎn)
drop

挑
(tiù / tiu¹) (tiāo)
tick

The word 永 (wíhng / wing[5]) (yǒng), meaning "forever" has each of the above eight strokes in itself.

The order of the strokes is as follows:

The traditional way of handling a brush
to write Chinese characters.

The following table illustrates the variety of the shapes of a stroke and gives examples of how they appear in a character:

Stroke	Shape	Example
點 (drop)	、 、 ノ 丶	六 衫 小 米 忙 池
橫 (horizontal)	一	十
直 (vertical)	丨	木
撇 (right falling slope)	ノ 丿 丿	人 井 菜
捺 (left falling slope)	丶 ㇏	大 是
挑 (tick)	㇀	拉 城
彎 (elbow)	乛 丷 ㇄ て 丿 く 丿 乃	日 衣 山 朵 紅 女 名 吸
勾 (hook)	亅 乀 乛 丿 乛 乃 乚 乚 乀 乙 乀	河 心 弟 家 刀 孕 家 他 我 汽

To help you understand the order of the stroke, here are some basic rules for you to follow:

Rule one: From top to bottom

Rule two: From left to right

Rule three: First horizontal, then vertical

Rule four: First horizontal,
                 then right falling slope

Rule five: First right falling slope,
              then left falling slope

Rule six: From outside to inside

Rule seven: Go inside then close the door

Rule eight: First middle, then preserve the symmetry

水 ➡ 亅 才 水

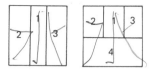

Apart from the above eight general rules, there are two more additional rules:

Rule nine: Three ways of writing dots

9a.   Write the dot first when it is on the left

斗 ➡ 丶 斗

9b.   Write the dot last when it is inside

寸 ➡ 十 寸

9c.   Write the dot last when it is on the top right

我 ➡ 我 我

Rule ten: First top right, then bottom left
            (usually for the radical 辶 or 廴)

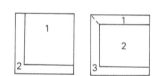

近 ➡ 斤 近

Chinese has many words which do not obey these rules. Pen order is not as simple as it seems! For these characters there is no choice but to remember their pen order by heart. For example, 水 (water) starts with the middle first and finishes with the strokes on the left and right. In contrast, the word 坐 (sit) is constructed by writing the left and right portions before the middle.

The Cantonese Sounds and Tones

Cantonese is a monosyllabic language that each word has only a single syllable. The various meanings of the each word are largely determined by the tone with which the word is pronounced.

Intonation is essential in reading Chinese because even if you produce the correct sound, associating it with a wrong tone can be a serious mistake: it will change the intended meaning. Good tones are life-time assets for Chinese language speakers.

A syllable in Cantonese has three elements:
1.   an initial, the beginning consonant
2.   a final, the ending of a syllable
3.   a tone, the pitch level of the syllable

Cantonese has seven tones. Since most speakers do not distinguish between the high level and high falling tones, we commonly consider only 6 basic Cantonese tones as follows:

Tones	High Falling	Middle Rising	Middle Level	Low Falling	Low Rising	Low Level
Tone No.	1	2	3	4	5	6
Pitch Level Chart (5–1)	↘	↗	→	↘	↗	→
	(5→3)	(3→5)	(3→3)	(2→1)	(2→3)	(2→2)
Lau	foo¹	foo²	foo³	foo⁴	foo⁵	foo⁶
Yale	fù	fú	fu	fùh	fúh	fuh
Chinese	夫	苦	褲	符	婦	父
English meaning	husband	bitter	trousers	charm	woman	father

N.B.   An * is used in the pronunciation systems to modify a tone in such a way that it is pronounced as in level 2.

There are 19 initials in Cantonese characters as illustrated in the following table:

Initial	Yale	Lau	Chinese	English
b	bà	ba[1]	爸	father
ch	chà	cha[1]	叉	fork
d	dà	da[1]	打	dozen
f	fà	fa[1]	花	flower
g	gà	ga[1]	家	home
gw	gwà	gwa[1]	瓜	melon
h	hà	ha[1]	蝦	shrimp
j	jì	ji[1]	知	to know
k	kà	ka[1]	卡	carat
kw	kwà	kwa[1]	誇	to exaggerate
l	làai	laai[1]	拉	to pull
m	mà	ma[1]	媽	mother
n	neíh	nei[5]	你	you
ng	ńg	ng[5]	五	five
p	paak	paak[3]	泊	to park (car)
s	sà	sa[1]	沙	sand
t	tà	ta[1]	他	he or she
w	wà	wa[1]	蛙	frog
y	yìn	yin[1]	煙	smoke

The Lau system has 53 Cantonese finals, which can be categorised into 9 groups:

1. **Group "a"**

Finals	as in
a	fast
ai	bite
au	pout
am	hum
an	sun
ang	rung
ap	sup
at	but
ak	duck

2. **Group "aa"**

Finals	as in
aai	island
aau	cow
aam	arm
aan	aunt
aang	aan + ng
aap	harp
aat	art
aak	ark

3. **Group "e"**

Finals	as in
e	merry
eng	length
ek	peck
ei	say
euh	her
eung	earn
euk	work

4. **Group "i"**

Finals	as in
i	bee
iu	ee + oo
im	seem
in	seen
ing	sing
ip	jeep
it	heat
ik	thick

5. **Group "o"**

Finals	as in
oh	saw
on	lawn
ot	bought
o	so
oi	toy
ong	long
ok	rock

6. **Group "oo"**

Finals	as in
oo	food
ooi	ruin
oon	noon
oot	foot

7. Group "u"

Finals	as in
ui	deuil*
un	nation
ut	put
ung	tongue
uk	took

8. Group "ue"

Finals	as in
ue	she
uen	tune
uet	parachute

9. Group Nasal

Finals	as in
m	mm
ng	singing

* No English equivalent, Pronouce in French

The Tones of Putonghua

The tone system of Putonghua is not as complicated as that of Cantonese. There are four tones in Putonghua. The range of variation of pitch is represented by four degrees as shown in the following table:

Tone	high level	high rising	low dipping	high falling
Symbol				
Pitch level chart (5 4 3 2 1)				
Tone pitch	5→5	3→5	2→1→4	5→1
Example	媽	麻	馬	罵
Pinyin	mā	má	mǎ	mà
English meaning	mother	trouble	horse	scold

Unit 1

yàhn   man
yan⁴   person
rén   human

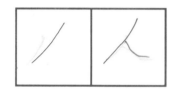

例句： 今天他休息，不來工作。

Example: Today he is on leave. He won't come to work.

(Yale)   Gàm tìn tà yàu sìk, bàt loih gùng jok.

(Lau)   Gam¹ tin¹ ta¹ yau¹ sik¹, bat¹ loi⁶ gung¹ jok⁶.

(Pinyin)   Jīn tiān tā xiū xī, bù lái gōng zuò.

Radical

The man standing upright indicates a relationship with people.

	Yale Lau	Pinyin	English
仔 *	jái jai²	zǎi	son
住	jyuh ju⁶	zhù	live
信	suen suen³	xìn	believe, trust
做	jouh jo⁶	zuò	do, make
來	loih loi⁶	lái	come
傘	san san³	sǎn	umbrella
他	tà ta¹	tā	he
他們	tà mùhn ta¹ moon⁴	tā men	they
今天	gàm tìn gam¹ tin¹	jīn tiān	today
你	néih nei⁵	nǐ	you (s.)
你們	néih mùhn nei⁵ moon⁴	nǐ men	you (pl.)
休息	yàu sìk yau¹ sik¹	xiū xǐ	rest
人工	yàhn gùng yan⁴ gung¹	rén gōng	salary

* 仔   is a Cantonese colloquialism.

Activity 1:   Write the Chinese Characters.

丿 人   man

人	人	人	人	人	人	人
人	人	人	人	人	人	

亻 仔 仔   son

仔	仔	仔	仔			

亻 什 休   门 自 息

休 息	休 息	休 息				

术 癶 来 來   come

來	來	來	來			

16

亻 仲 他 ?

他						

亻 伊 佴 佴 們 you? or plural?

們	們	們	們	們	們	們

亻 仜 佇 你 you single.

你	你	你	你			

人 仐 仐 傘 umbrella.

傘	傘	傘				

Activity 2:   Match the Chinese vocabulary with the English meaning.

他們 • 4   • rest 4

做 • 5   • come 5

今天 • 3   • today 3

休息 • 1   • they 1

來 • 2   • do, make 2

Activity 3:   Fill in the missing Chinese characters to complete the words.

1.
今 天

today

2.
你 們

you (pl.)

3.
住

live

4.
亻

trust

5.
人

umbrella

6.
亻 息

rest

Unit 2

dòu
do¹
dāo

knife

例句： 媽媽用刀切水果。

Example: Mother uses a knife to cut the fruit.

(Yale)   Mà mà yuhng dòu chit séui gwó.

(Lau)   Ma¹ ma¹ yung⁶ do¹ chit³ sui² gwoh².

(Pinyin)   Mā mā yòng dāo qiē shuǐ guǒ.

Radical

This radical indicates a relationship with knives or something sharp.

	Yale Lau	Pinyin	English
刀	dòu do¹	dāo	*knife*
切	chit chit³	qiē	*cut*
利	leih lei⁶	lí	*sharp*
分	fàn fan¹	fēn	*separate, divide*
別	biht bit⁶	bié	*depart*
到	dou do³	dào	*arrive*
刺	chi chi³	cì	*stab*
刻	hàk hak¹	kè	*carve*
前	chìhn chin⁴	qián	*front*
初	chò choh¹	chū	*beginning (n.)*
劍	gim gim³	jian	*sword*
剪刀	jín dòu jin² do¹	jiǎn dāo	*scissors*

Activity 1:   Write the Chinese Characters.

フ 刀

刀							

八 分

分							

一 七 切 切

切							

千 禾 利

利							

分 ㄅ ㄇ 丹 别

分	别						

工 至 到

到							

冂 巾 朿 刺

刺							

亠 首 前 剪 刀

剪	刀						

Activity 2:   Match the Chinese vocabulary with the English meaning.

分 •   • carve

到 •   • divide

利 •   • sharp

切 •   • cut

刻 •   • arrive

Activity 3: Write the suitable Chinese characters to match the pictures.

1.

_____ _____

2.

_____

3.

_____

4.

_____

別   剪刀   分   切

23

Unit 3

 háu
hau²
kŏu

mouth

opening

例句: 我用口唱歌，吃飯和吹口哨。

Example: I use (my) mouth to sing songs, eat rice and whistle.

(Yale)   Ngóh yuhng háu cheung gò, hèt faahn, wóh cheùi háu saau.

(Lau)   Ngoh⁵ yung⁶ hau² cheung³ goh¹, het³ faan⁶ wo⁵ chui¹ hau²
            saau³.

(Pinyin)   Wǒ yòng kŏu chàng gē, chī fàn hé chuī kŏu shào.

Radical

The square indicates a relationship with the mouth.
It also signifies an opening.

24

	Yale Lau	Pinyin	English
入口	yahp háu yap⁶ hau²	rù kǒu	entrance
出口	chùt háu chut¹ hau²	chū kǒu	exit
口渴	háu hot hau² hot⁶	kǒu kě	thirsty
吵	cháu chau²	chǎo	quarrel
味	meih mei⁶	wèi	taste
吻	máhn man⁵	wěn	kiss
唱歌	cheung gò cheung³ goh¹	chàng gē	sing songs
吹	chèui cheui¹	chuī	blow
問	mahn man⁶	wèn	ask
叫	giu giu³	jiào	shout
吃	het het³	chī	eat
咬	ngáauh ngaau⁵	yǎo	bite
喝	hot hot⁶	hē	drink
哈哈	hà hà ha¹ ha¹	hā hā	ha ha (laugh)

Activity 1:   Write the Chinese Characters.

丶 冂 口

口							

口 吻 吻

吻							

口 唱 唱

唱							

口 吹 吹

吹							

口 叱 吃

吃							

口 叭 吟 哈

哈							

卩 卩丨 卩比 門 問

問							

口 叮 叫

叫							

Activity 2: **What are these people doing?**

1.

_____

2.

_____

3.

_____

4.

_____

5.

_____

6.

_____

Activity 3: **What do you do when you are:**

1. in love   (   )

2. happy   (   )

3. hungry   (   )

4. in doubt   (   )

5. in a karaoke lounge   (   )

Unit 4

tóu
to²
tǔ

land

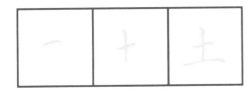

例句： 地上有一本地址簿。

Example: There is an address book on the ground.

(Yale)   Deih seuhng yáuh yàt bún deih jí bóu.

(Lau)   Dei⁶ seung⁶ yau⁵ yat¹ boon² dei⁶ ji² bo⁶*.

(Pinyin)   Dì shàng yǒu yī běn dì zhǐ bù.

Radical

 ， ，

This radical indicates a relationship with land or ground.

	Yale Lau	Pinyin	English
地	deih dei⁶	dì	*ground, land, floor*
地址	deih jí dei⁶ ji²	dì zhǐ	*address*
坐	joh jo⁶, choh⁵	zuò	*sit*
埋	màaih maai⁴	mái	*bury*
城	sìhng sing⁴	chéng	*city*
填	tìhn tin⁴	tián	*fill in*
壞	waaih waai⁶	huài	*bad, rotten, out of order*
堅	gìn gin¹	jiān	*strong*
塵	chàhn chan⁴	chén	*dust*
一堆	yàht dèui yat¹ deui¹	yī duī	*a heap*
一塊	yàht faai yat¹ faai³	yī kuài	*a piece*
場地	chèuhng deih cheung⁴ dei⁶	cháng dì	*venue*
基本	geì bún gei¹ boon²	jī běn	*basic*
大堂	daaih tòhng dai⁶ tong⁴	dà táng	*hall*

Activity 1:   Write the Chinese Characters.

一 十 土

土							

土 圠 坳 地

地							

地   土 圤 圤 址

地	址						

人 从 坐

坐							

土 坦 坤 埋

埋							

土 圠 圻 城 城 城

城							

一 土 坤 塊 塊

一	塊						

一 土 圵 堆 堆

一	堆						

Activity 2:   Match the Chinese vocabulary with the English meaning.

一堆 ·   · sit

城 ·   · floor

坐 ·   · city

一块 ·   · a piece

地 ·   · a heap

Activity 3: Write the suitable Chinese characters to match the pictures.

1.

2.

_____ _____   _____

3.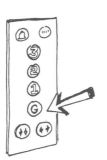

4.

_____   _____

Unit 5

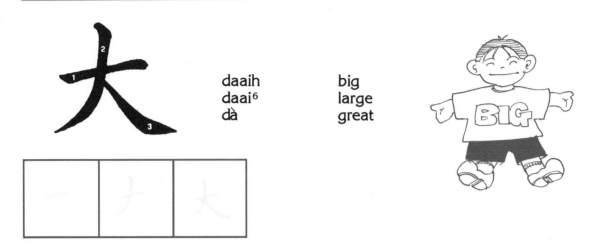

daaih
daai[6]
dà

big
large
great

例句: 李太太每天在大廈裏大聲唱歌，
奇怪！真奇怪！

Example: Everyday Mrs Lee sings loudly in the mansion. (It is) strange!
             really strange!

(Yale)   Léih taai táai* muih tìn joih daaih hah léuih daaih sìng cheung
             gò, kèih gwaai! jàn kèih gwaai!

(Lau)   Lei[5] taai[3] taai[3]* mooi[5] tin[1] joi[6] daai[6] ha[6] lui[5] daai[6] sing[1] cheung[3]
             goh[1], kei[4] kwaai[3]! jan[1] kei[4] gwaai[3]!

(Pinyin)   Lǐ tài tài měi tiān zài dà shà lǐ dà shēng chàng gē, qí quài! zhēn
             qí quài!

Radical

This radical can stand on its own and always means big, large and great.

	Yale Lau	Pinyin	English
太太	taai táai* taai³ taai³*	tài tài	*Mrs.; wife*
天	tìn tin¹	tiān	*day, sky*
獎	jéung jeung²	jiǎng	*prize*
每天	muih tìn mooi⁵ tin¹	měi tiān	*everyday*
奇怪	kèih gwaai kei⁴ gwaai³	qí quài	*strange*
大家	daaih gà daai⁶ ga¹	dà jiā	*all of us*
大人	daaih yàhn daai⁶ yan⁴	dà rén	*big man (adult)*
大廈	daaih hah daai⁶ ha⁶	dà shà	*mansion*
大學	daaih hohk daai⁶ hok⁶	dà xué	*university*
大力	daaih lihk daai⁶ lik⁶	dà lì	*full of strength*
大約	daaih yeuk daai⁶ yeuk³	dà yuē	*approximately*
大聲	daaih sìng daai⁶ sing¹	dà shēng	*loud*
大減價	daaih gáam ga daai⁶ gaam² ga³	dà jiǎn jià	*big sale*

Activity 1:   Write the Chinese Characters.

一 ナ 大

大							

大 太

太							

二 天

天							

大 フ カ

大	力						

大　宀宀宀宇家家

大	家						

大　卢臼臼臼學學

大	學						

大　幺糸約約約

大	約						

大　士声声殸聲

大	聲				

Activity 2: Match the Chinese vocabulary with the English meaning.

大聲 •   • everybody

大力 •   • strong

大學 •   • mansion

大家 •   • loud

大廈 •   • university

Activity 3: Put the words in the correct order to make complete sentences

1) 車裏火熱炎很。

_____

2) 很大家怪奇。

_____

3) 天在學他天大飯吃。

_____

4) 天大息今家休。

_____

Unit 6

síu
siu²
xiǎo

small

young

例句： 李小姐在小巴裏看小説。

Example: Miss Lee is reading a novel in the minibus.

(Yale)   Léih síu jé joih síu bà léuih hon síu syut.

(Lau)   Lei⁵ siu² je² joi⁶ siu² ba¹ lui⁵ hon³ siu² suet³.

(Pinyin)   Lǐ xiǎo jiě zài xiǎo bā lǐ kàn xiǎo shuō.

Radical

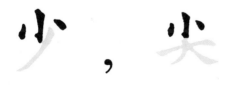

This radical can stand on its own, meaning small.

	Yale Lau	Pinyin	English
大小	daaih síu daai⁶ siu²	dà xiǎo	*big and small*
多少	dò síu doh¹ siu²	duō shǎo	*how much?*
多多少少	dò dò síu síu doh¹ doh¹ siu² siu²	duō duō shǎo shǎo	*more or less*
尖	jìm jim¹	jiān	*sharp*
小心	síu sàm siu² sam¹	xiǎo xīn	*be careful*
小姐	síu jé siu² je²	xiǎo jiě	*Miss, lady*
小説	síu syut siu² suet³	xiǎo shuō	*fiction, novel*
小偷	síu tàu siu² tau¹	xiǎo tōu	*thief*
小學	síu hohk siu² hok⁶	xiǎo xué	*primary school*
小販	síu faan siu² faan³	xiǎo fàn	*street hawker*
小巴	síu bà siu² ba¹	xiǎo bā	*mini-bus*

Activity 1:   Write the Chinese Characters.

丿 亅 小

小							

小   フ ヲ ヱ 巴

小	巴						

小   臼 段 樹 幽 學

小	學						

丿 勹 夕 多   少

多	少						

小 尖

尖							

小 女 如 姐 姐

小	姐						

小 言 訁 説 説

小	説						

小 亻 伀 伀 偷 偷

小	偷						

Activity 2: Write the suitable Chinese vocabulary under each picture.

1.

_____

2.

_____

3.

_____

4.

_____

5.

_____

6.

_____ _____

7.

_____ _____

8.

_____ _____

Unit 7

néuih   woman
nui⁵   girl
nǔ   daughter

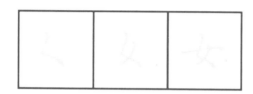

例句: 我有一子一女，我妻子是家裏
的女王。

Example: I have one son (and) one daughter. My wife is the queen in the family.

(Yale)   Ngóh yáuh yàt jí yàt néuih, ngóh chài jí shih gà néuih dǐk néuih wòhng.

(Lau)   Ngoh⁵ yau⁵ yat¹ ji² yat¹ nui⁵, ngoh⁵ chai¹ ji² si⁶ ga¹ lui⁵ dik¹ nui⁵ wong⁴.

(Pinyin)   Wǒ yǒu yī zǐ yī nǔ, wǒ qī zǐ shì jiā lǐ dì nǔ wáng.

Radical

 女 ， 女

This radical indicates a relationship with female.

	Yale Lau	Pinyin	English
女人	neuih yán nui⁵ yan⁴•	nǔ rén	woman
女王	néuih wòhng nui⁵ wong⁴	nǔ wáng	queen
女朋友	néuih pèhng yáuh nui⁵ pang⁴ yau⁵	nǔ péng yǒu	girl friend
奶	náaih naai⁵	nǎi	milk
她	tà ta¹	tā	she
好	hóu ho²	hǎo	good *(one daughter and one son must be good)*
姊	jí ji²	zǐ	elder sister
妹	múi mooi⁶•	mèi	younger sister
媽	mà ma¹	mā	mother
婆	pòh poh⁴	pó	grandmother
妻子	chài jí chai¹ ji²	qī zǐ	wife
姓	sing sing³	xìng	surname
姑	gù gu¹	gū	aunt
姦	gàain gaain¹	jiān	rape

Activity 1:   Write the Chinese Characters.

く 夕 女

女							

女　月 朋　ナ 方 友

女	朋	友					

女 奵 好

好							

女 奵 奵 她

她							

女ˊ 奻 姉 姉

姉							

女 女= 妹 妹

妹							

女 奻 姓 姓　ク 夕 名

姓	名						

女 奻 妡 姮 媽

媽							

Activity 2:   **Match the Chinese vocabulary with the English meaning.**

媽 •   • elder sister

姊 •   • younger sister

妹 •   • mother

她 •   • good

好 •   • she

Activity 3:   **Talk to four friends. Write down their names in the first column. Then ask them:**

a.   Whether they are married? (結婚）

b.   If they have girl friends? (女朋友)

c.   How many elder sisters they have? (姊)

d.   How many younger sisters they have? (妹)

e.   How many children they have? (子女)

姓名	結婚	女朋友	姊	妹	子女

Unit 8

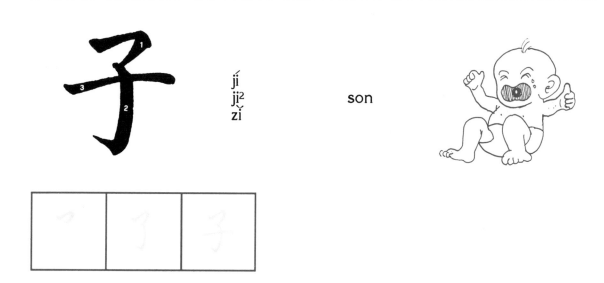

子

jí
jí²
zǐ

son

例句: 李太太的孩子在學校裏學寫字。

Example: Mrs. Lee's children are learning writing in school.

(Yale)   Léih taai táai* dìk hàaih jí jóih hohk haauh léuih hohk sé jí.

(Lau)   Lei⁵ taai³ taai³* dik¹ haai⁴ ji² joi⁵ hok⁶ haau⁶ lui⁵ hok⁶ se² ji².

(Pinyin)   Lǐ tài tài dì hái zǐ zài xué xiào lǐ xué xiě zì.

Radical

This radical indicates a relationship with children or people.

49

Vocabulary

	Yale Lau	Pinyin	English
子女	jí néuih ji² nui⁵	zǐ nǔ	children
孩子	hàaih jí haai⁴ ji²	hái zǐ	little boy or girl
男子	nàahm jí naam⁴ ji²	nán zǐ	male
女子	néuih jí nui⁵ ji²	nǔ zǐ	female
仔 *	jái jai²	zǎi	son
字	ji ji⁶	zì	word
孕	yahn yan⁶	yùn	pregnant
孫	syùn suen¹	sūn	grandchildren
學	hohk hok⁶	xué	learn, study

* 仔   is a Cantonese colloquialism.

Activity 1:   Write the Chinese Characters.

`ㄱ  了  子`

子

`ㄥ  女  女    子`

女 子

`田  男    子`

男 子

`孑  孖  孩  孩  孩    子`

孩 子

ㄅ 字

字

ㄅ 乃 孕

孕

ㄋ ㄋˊ 孫 孫

孫

ㅏ 段 學 學 學

學

Activity 2: Match the Chinese vocabulary with the English meaning.

學   •   •   pregnant

孩   •   •   word

孕   •   •   child

字   •   •   learn

孫   •   •   grandchild

Activity 3: Fill in the missing Chinese characters to complete the words.

1.

子

grandchild

2.

子

word

3.

子

child

4.

子

learn

5.

亻

son

6.

子

pregnant

53

Unit 9

sàm
sam[1]
xīn

heart

例句： 小息時，我們在語言中心吃
點心。大家要小心。

Example: During recess, we eat dim sum in the Language Centre. All of
us should be careful. (Don't drop any food on the floor!)

(Yale)   Síu sìk sìh, ngóh mùhn joih yúh yìhn jùng sàm hek dím sàm.
Daaih gà yiu síu sàm.

(Lau)   Siu[2] sik[1] si[4] ngoh[5] moon[4] joi[6] yue[5] yin[4] jung[1] sam[1] hek[3] dim[2]
sam[1]. Daai[6] ga[1] yiu[3] siu[2] sam[1].

(Pinyin)   Xiǎo xī shí, wǒ men zài yǔ yán zhōng xīn chī diǎn xīn. Dà jiā
yào xiǎo xīn.

Radical

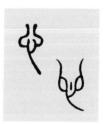

This radical indicates a relationship with the heart.

	Yale Lau	Pinyin	English
中心	jùng sàm jung¹ sam¹	zhōng xīn	centre
心中	sàm jùng sam¹ jung¹	xīn zhōng	in the heart
小心	síu sàm siu² sam¹	xiǎo xīn	careful
點心	dím sàm dim² sam¹	diǎn xīn	dim sum
必要	bì yiu bi¹ yiu³	bì yào	must
忙	mòhng mong⁴	máng	busy
忘	mòhng mong⁴	wàng	forget
恐怕	húng pa hung² pa³	kǒng pà	afraid
思想	sì séung si¹ seung²	sī xiǎng	think, thought (n.)
急	gàp gap¹	jí	urgent
快	faai faai³	kuài	quick
怪	gwai gwai³	guài	strange
恨你	hahn néih han⁶ nei⁵	hèn nǐ	hate you
小息	síu sìk siu² sik¹	xiǎo xī	little rest, recess

Activity 1:   Write the Chinese Characters.

丶 心 心 心

心							

口 中 心

中	心						

口 甲 里 黑 點 心

點	心						

丶 忄 忄 忙 忙 忙

忙							

一 亡 忘

忘							

忄 忄 快

快							

木 相 想

想							

勹 勺 刍 急

急							

Activity 2: Fill in the brackets with suitable Chinese words that correspond to the English meaning.

a. 我 （　　　） 你。

I <u>think</u> of you

b. 我 （　　　） 你。

I <u>hate</u> you.

c. 我 很 （　　　） 。

I am very <u>busy</u>.

d. 我很 （　　） 吃 （　　　）（　　　）。

I eat <u>dim sum</u> <u>quickly</u>.

e. 我 （　　）（　　） 去 （　　） （　　）
學中文。

I <u>must</u> go to the <u>Centre</u> to learn Chinese.

f. 我是 （　　） 人，他是 （　　　） 人。

I am a <u>good</u> (nice) person. He is a <u>strange</u> person.

Unit 10

sáu
sau²
shǒu

hand

The palm lines on the hand;
five fingers on the hand.

例句: 我去洗手間洗手。

Example: I go to the washroom to wash hands.

(Yale)   Ngóh heui sái sáu gàan sái sáu.

(Lau)   Ngoh⁵ hui³ sai² sau² gaan¹ sai² sau².

(Pinyin)   Wǒ qù xǐ shǒu jiān xǐ shǒu.

Radical

This radical indicates a relationship with hands.

	Yale Lau	Pinyin	English
手指	sáu jí sau² ji²	shǒu zhǐ	*finger*
手表	sáu bìu sau² biu¹	shǒu biǎo	*wrist-watch*
手巾	sáu gàng sau² gang¹	shǒu jīn	*towel, handkerchief*
手套	sáu tou sau² to³	shǒu tào	*gloves*
洗手間	sái sáu gàan sai² sau² gaan¹	xǐ shǒu jiān	*washroom*
打	dá da²	dǎ	*hit, beat*
抄	chàau chaau¹	chāo	*copy*
折	jit jit³	zhé	*break*
八折	ba jit baat³ jit³	bā zhé	*20% discount*
捉	jùk juk¹	zhuō	*catch*
拉	làai laai¹	lā	*pull*
推	tèui teui¹	tuī	*push*
抱	póuh po⁵	bào	*hold*
掌	jéung jeung²	zhǎng	*palm*

Activity 1: Write the Chinese Characters.

丿 二 三 手

手							

手 扌 扗 指

手	指						

氵 汫 洗 　 手 　 阝 阼 門 間

洗	手	間					

扌 打

打							

才 抄 抄

抄							

才 扣 押 捉

捉							

才 扩 拉 拉

拉							

才 扩 推 推

推							

Activity 2:   Write the Chinese vocabulary under each picture.

1.

_____ _____

2.

_____ _____

3.

_____ _____

4.

_____

5.

_____

6.

_____

Unit 11

 yaht
yat[6]
rì

sun

day

例句: 哥哥昨日早上寫字，晚上唱歌。

Example: (My) elder brother did some writing yesterday morning, (and) sang in the evening.

(Yale) Gò gò jok yaht jó seuhng sé jí, máahn seuhng cheung gò.

(Lau) Goh[1] goh[1] jok[6] yat[6] jo[2] seung[6] se[2] ji[2], maan[5] seung[6] cheung[3] goh[1].

(Pinyin) Gē gē zuó rì zao shàng xiě zǐ, wǎn shàng chàng gē.

Radical

 ,

This radical indicates a relationship with the sun.

	Yale Lau	Pinyin	English
日期	yaht kèih yat⁶ kei⁴	rì qī	*date*
早上	jó seuhng jo² seung⁶	zǎo shàng	*in the morning*
早晨	jó sàhn jo² san⁴	zǎo chén	*good morning*
昌明	chèung mìhng cheung¹ ming⁴	chāng míng	*prosperous*
昨日	jok yaht jok⁶ yat⁶	zuó rì	*yesterday*
昨晚	jok máahn jok⁶ maan⁵	zuó wǎn	*last night*
明日	mìhng yaht ming⁴ yat⁶	míng rì	*tomorrow*
明白	mìhng bahk ming⁴ baak⁶	míng bái	*understand*
春天	chùn tìn chun¹ tin¹	chūn tiān	*spring*
晴	chìhng ching⁴	qíng	*sunny*
是	sih si⁶	shì	*is, am, are*
小時	síu sìh siu² si⁴	xiǎo shí	*hour*
亮晶晶	leuh jìng jìng leung⁶ jing¹ jing¹	liàng jīng jīng	*shinny, bright*
星期日	sìng kèih yaht sing¹ kei⁴ yat⁶	xīng qī rì	*Sunday*

Activity 1:   Write the Chinese Characters.

丨 冂 月 日

日							

日 早   丨 卜 上

早	上						

早   日 尸 层 晨 晨

早	晨						

日 旷 旷 昨   日

昨	日						

日 明　ノ 竹 白

明	白						

日 旱 早 是

是							

小　日 旪 時 時

小	時						

尸 旦 星　廿 甘 其 期　日

星	期	日					

Activity 2:   Match the Chinese vocabulary with the English meaning.

一星期   •   • tomorrow

星期一   •   • understand

小時   •   • one week

明白   •   • Monday

明日   •   • yesterday

昨日   •   • today

今日   •   • hour

Activity 3:   Fill in the blanks with suitable Chinese.

1. 今日（   ）星期三。

2. （   ）（   ）是星期四。

3. （   ）（   ）（   ）星期二。

4. 一日有24（   ）（   ）。

5. 一（   ）（   ）有 7日。

Unit 12

yuht
yuet[6]
yuè

moon
month

例句：　月光下，我請朋友吃月餅。

Example:	In the moonlight, I treat (my) friend to eat moon cake.
(Yale)	Yuht gwòng hak, ngóh chíng pàhng yáuh hek yuht béng.
(Lau)	Yuet[6] gwong[1] ha[6], ngoh[5] cheng[2] pang[4] yau[5] hek[3] yuet[6] beng[2].
(Pinyin)	Yuè guāng xià, wǒ qǐng péng yǒu chī yuè bǐng.

Radical

 ， ，

This radical can stand on its own, meaning the moon or month.

	Yale Lau	Pinyin	English
月餅	yuht béng yuet⁶ beng²	yuè bǐng	mooncake
有	yáuh yau⁵	yǒu	have, has, there is
朋友	pàhng yáuh pang⁴ yau⁵	péng yǒu	friend
日期	yaht kèih yat⁶ kei⁴	rì qī	date
晴朗	chìhng lóhng cheng⁴ long⁵	qíng lǎng	bright and sunny
衣服	yì fuhk yi¹ fuk⁶	yī fú	clothes
月光	yuht gwong yuet⁶ gwong¹	yuè guāng	moonlight
月亮	yuht leuhng yuet⁶ lueng⁶	yuè liàng	moon
二月	yi yuht yi⁶ yuet⁶	èr yuè	February
三月	sàam yuht saam¹ yuet⁶	sān yuè	March
四月	sei yuht sei³ yuet⁶	sì yuè	April
五月	ńg yuht ng⁵ yuet⁶	wǔ yuè	May
六月	luhk yuhk luk⁶ yuet⁶	liù yuè	June
七月	chàt yuhk chat¹ yuet⁶	qī yuè	July

Activity 1:   Write the Chinese Characters.

） 几 月 月

月							

月　八 今 食 飣 餅

月	餅						

广 有

有							

月 朋　广 友

朋	友					

日　廾　其　期

日	期					

日　日ˉ　日ᵗ　旺　晴　　彐　良　朗　朗

晴	朗					

亠　广　衣　　月　月ˊ　明　服

衣	服					

月　　丨　⺌　光

月	光					

Activity 2: Match the Chinese vocabulary with the English meaning.

月亮 •   • moon

月餅 •   • moonlight

朋友 •   • mooncake

衣服 •   • sunny and bright

月光 •   • clothes

Activity 3: Put the words in the correct order to make complete sentences.

1. 月餅我明吃天。

   _____

2. 是的好我朋友她 。

   _____

3. 氣昨晴朗日天 。

   _____

4. 月三日三有一十。

   _____

73

Unit 13

muhk
muk[6]
mù

wood

tree

例句： 森林裏，樹木多，可以做木材。

Example: In a jungle, there are lots of trees. (We) can use (them) for
            timber.

(Yale)   Sàm làhm léuih, syuh muhk dò, hó yíh jouh muhk chòih.

(Lau)   Sam[1] lam[4] lui[5], sue[6] muk[6] doh[1], hoh[2] yi[5] jo[6] muk[6] choi[4].

(Pinyin)   Sēn lín lǐ, shù mù duō, kě yǐ zuò mù cái.

Radical

The tree with its branches, trunk and roots indicates
a relationship with wood.

	Yale Lau	Pinyin	English
木材	muhk chòih muk⁶ choi⁴	mù cái	*timber*
森林	sàm làhm sam¹ lam⁴	sēn lín	*jungle*
樹林	syuh làhm sue⁶ lam⁴	shù lín	*forest*
樹木	syuh muhk sue⁶ muk⁶	shù mù	*tree*
本	bún boon²	běn	*base*
杯	bùi booi¹	bēi	*cup, mug*
村	chyùn chuen¹	cūn	*village*
根	gàn gan¹	gēn	*root*
橙	chàang chaang⁴	chéng	*orange*
桃	tòuh to⁴	táo	*peach*
檯(枱)*	tòih toi⁴	tái	*table*
橋	kìuh kiu⁴	qiáo	*bridge*
果	gwó gwoh²	guǒ	*fruit*
梨	lèih lei⁴	lí	*pear*

* 檯 is usually written as 枱 for convenience.

Activity 1:   Write the Chinese Characters.

一 十 才 木

木

木 术 森 林

森 林

木 杜 桔 樹 樹

樹

木 杞 椺 根

根

木 杧 杯

杯							

木 杧 村

村							

木 杧 桃 橙

橙							

木 木 村 材

木	材						

Activity 2:   Write the suitable Chinese vocabulary to match the pictures.

1.

_____

2.

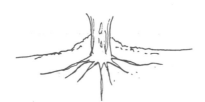

_____

3.

_____

4.

_____

5.

_____

6.

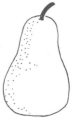

_____

Activity 3:   Match the Chinese vocabulary with the English meaning.

森林 •   • timber

樹木 •   • tree

樹林 •   • forest

木材 •   • jungle

78

Unit 14

séui
sui²
shuǐ

water

例句：今天天氣很好，我們去游泳。

Example: Today the weather is fine, we go swimming.

(Yale)   Gàm tìn tìn hei háng hóu, ngóh mùhn heui yàuh wihng.

(Lau)   Gam¹ tin¹ tin¹ hei³ hang² ho², ngoh⁵ moon⁴ hui³ yau⁴ wing⁶.

(Pinyin)   Jīn tiān tiān qǐ hěn hǎo, wǒ men qù yóu yǒng.

Radical

Three drops of water indicate a relationship with water.

	Yale Lau	Pinyin	English
汗	hohn hon⁶	hàn	sweat
河	hòh hoh⁴	hé	river
汽水	hei séui hei³ sui²	qì shuǐ	soft drink
果汁	gwó jàp gwoh² jap¹	guǒ zhī	fruit juice
洗	sái sai²	xǐ	wash
洗面	sái mihn sai² min⁶	xǐ miàn	wash face
淚	luih lui⁶	lèi	tear (n.)
海	hói hoi²	hǎi	sea
海洋	hói yèuhng hoi² yeung⁴	hǎi yáng	ocean
湯	tòng tong¹	tāng	soup
淺	chín chin²	qiǎn	shallow
深	sàm sam¹	shēn	deep
游泳	yàuh wihng yau⁴ wing⁶	yóu yǒng	swim
游泳池	yàuh wihng chi yau⁴ wing⁶ chi³	yóu yǒng chí	swimming pool

Activity 1:　Write the Chinese Characters.

丨 刀 水

水							

氵 汽 汽

汽	水						

氵 汒 汰 海 海 海

海							

氵 汒 洪 洗

洗							

氵 汇 河 河

河

氵 汇 池 池

池

氵 汁

汁

氵 汇 深 深 深

深

Avtivity 2:   Match the Chinese vocabulary with the English meaning.

1. 游泳 （　　）
2. 河　　（　　）
3. 汽水 （　　）
4. 洗面 （　　）
5. 水果 （　　）
6. 果汁 （　　）

a.

b.

c.

d.

e.

f.

Activity 3:   Fill in the missing Chinese characters to complete the words.

1.
氵

sweat

2.
氵水

soft drink

3.
氵

soup

4.
氵

wash

5.
氵

deep

6.
氵

juice

Unit 15

fó
foh²
huǒ

fire

例句: 火車在火炭站死火，很麻煩。

Example: The train is broken down in Fotan Station. (It is) very troublesome.

(Yale) Fó chè joih Fó Táan jaahm séi fó, háng màh fàahn.

(Lau) Foh² che¹ joi⁶ Foh² Tan² jaam⁶ sei² foh², hang² ma⁴ faan⁴.

(Pinyin) Huǒ chē zài Huǒ Tàn zhàn sǐ huǒ, hěn má fán.

Radical

 ，  ， 熱

This radical indicates a relationship with fire.

	Yale Lau	Pinyin	English
火車	fó chè foh² che¹	huǒ chē	*train*
死火*	séi fó sei² foh²	sǐ huǒ	*broken down*
炎熱	yìhm yiht yim⁴ yit⁶	yán rè	*very hot*
炒	cháau chaau²	chǎo	*stir fry*
炭	taan taan³	tàn	*charcoal*
煩	fàahn fan⁴	fán	*troublesome*
煙	yìn yin¹	yān	*smoke, cigarette*
不准吸煙	bàt júen kàp yìn bat¹ juen² kap¹ yin¹	bù zhǔn xī yān	*no smoking*
燈	dàng dang¹	dēng	*lamp*
熟	suhk suk⁶	shú	*well cooked*
燒	sìu siu¹	shāo	*burn*
煮	jyú jue²	zhǔ	*cook*
煲	bòu bou¹	bāo	*boil, pot (n.)*

* 死火 *is a Cantonese colloquialism, not normally used by Putonghua speakers*

Activity 1:   Write the Chinese Characters.

丶 火

火							

火 炎   土 夫 幸 執 執 熱

炎	熱						

火 炒 炒

炒							

火 炉 煩 煩

煩							

火 炉 炬 炬 煙

煙							

火 灯 烃 燈

燈							

火 灶 烊 燒 燒

燒							

亻 伢 保 煲

煲							

Activity 2:   Match the Chinese vocabulary with the English meaning.

燈 •   • smoke

煮 •   • lamp

燒 •   • burn

煙 •   • cook

Activity 3:   Circle the vocabulary in the grid. The number in the brackets indicates the number of characters in the word.

死	火	炭	吸	煙	麻	煩
口	車	男	火	樹	木	燈
炎	女	人	森	林	口	芒
熱	炒	工	煮	汽	水	果

saliva (2)	fruit (2)	train (2)
steaming hot (2)	forest (2)	Fotan (2)
tree (2)	smoking (2)	broken down (2)
jungle(2)	numb (2)	cook (1)
fry (1)	soft drink (2)	troublesome (2)
salary (2)	man (2)	woman (2)

Unit 16

muhk
muk⁶   eye
mù

例句：我睡前喜歡看書。

Example: I like to read books and watch television before I sleep.

(Yale)   Ngóh seuih chìhn héi fùn hon syù.

(Lau)   Ngoh⁵ sui⁶ chin⁴ hei² foon¹ hon³ sue¹.

(Pinyin)   Wǒ shuì qián xǐ huān kàn shū.

Radical

 ， ，直 ，眾

This radical indicates a relationship with eyes.

Vocabulary

	Yale Lau	Pinyin	English
盲	màhng mang⁴	máng	*blind*
看	hon hon³	kàn	*look, read, watch*
真	jàn jan¹	zhēn	*real*
睡	seuih sui⁶	shuì	*sleep*
眉	mèih mei⁴	méi	*eye brow*
眼	ngáahn ngaan⁵	yǎn	*eye*
直	jihk jik⁶	zhí	*straight*
省	sáang saang²	shěng	*province*
相	seung seung³	xiāng	*photograph*
眾	jung jung³	zhòng	*crowd (of people)*
睇*	tái tai²	dì	*watch, read*
睇電視	tái dihn sih tai² din⁶ si⁶	dì dian shi	*watch TV.*

---

* 睇 *is a Cantonese colloquialism, Putonghua speakers use* 看 *.*

Activity 1:   Write the Chinese Characters.

丨 冂 冃 冃 目

目							

亠 亡 盲

盲							

三 チ 看

看							

目 旺 晅 睡 睡

睡							

十 直 直

直

十 直 真

真

日 日 目 眼 眼

眼

丷 丷 半 羊 着

着

Activity 2: Match the Chinese vocabulary with the English meaning.

省 •　　　• province

看 •　　　• read (formal)

盲 •　　　• blind

睡 •　　　• sleep

眼 •　　　• eye

Activity 3: Fill in the missing Chinese characters to complete the words.

1.

目

eye

2.

目

sleep

3.

木

photo

4.

目

look

5.

目

blind

6.

目

straight

Unit 17

 jùk
juk¹
zhú

bamboo

例句: 我用筆在簽名簿上簽名。

Example: I use a pen to sign (my) name on the signature book.

(Yale)   Ngóh yohng bàt joih chìm méng* bóu* seuhng chìm méng*.

(Lau)   Ngoh⁵ yung⁶ bat¹ joi⁶ chim¹ meng⁴* bo⁶* seung⁶ chim¹ meng⁴*.

(Pinyin)   Wǒ yòng bǐ zài qiān míng bù shàng qiān míng.

Radical

This radical indicates a relationship with bamboo.

	Yale Lau	Pinyin	English
笑	siu siu³	xiào	*laugh*
笨	bahn ban⁶	bèn	*stupid*
第一	daih yàt dai⁶ yat¹	dì yī	*number 1*
筆	bàt bat¹	bǐ	*pen*
答	daap daap³	dá	*answer*
計算	gai syun gai³ suen³	jì suàn	*calculate*
箱	sèung seung¹	xiāng	*box*
簽名	chìm méng• chim¹ meng⁴•	qiān	*sign, signature*
簿	bou bou⁶	bù	*book (for writing)*
籃	làahm laam⁴	lán	*basket*
籠	lùhng lung⁴	lóng	*cage*
等	dáng dang²	děng	*wait*
等一等	dáng yàt dáng dang² yat¹ dang²	děng yī děng	*wait a minute*

Activity 1: Write the Chinese Characters.

ㄟ 竹

竹							

⺮ 笑

笑							

⺮ 竺 等

等							

⺮ ⺮ 箔 簿 蒲 薄 薄

薄							

96

竹 竹 竿 筀 筆

筆							

竹 筲 箱

箱							

竹 筊 答

答							

筊 筊 答 簽　ク タ 名

簽	名						

Activity 2: Write the suitable Chinese character under each picture. You can choose the appropriate characters from the box below.

1.

_____

2.

_____

3.

_____

4.

_____

5.

no.3

_____

6.

_____

笑　第三　筆　計算　箱　簿

Unit 18

yì
yi[1]
yī

clothes

丶	亠	宀	衤	衣	衣

例句: 我在女裝部買了很多衣服，
有裙也有褲。

Example: I have bought lots of clothes in the Ladies' Department. (I have) dresses and trousers.

(Yale) Ngóh joih néuih jòng bouh máaih líuh háng dò yì fuhk, yáuh kwàhn yáh yáuh fu.

(Lau) Ngoh[5] joi[6] nui[5] jong[1] bo[6] maai[5] liu[5] hang[5] do[1] yi[1] fuk[6], yau[5] kwan[4] ya[5] yau[5] foo[3].

(Pinyin) Wǒ zài nǔ zhuāng bù mǎi liǎo hěn duō yī fú, yǒu qún yě yǒu kù.

 ,

This radical indicates a relationship with clothes.

	Yale Lau	Pinyin	English
衣服	yì fuhk yi¹ fuk⁶	yī fú	clothes
衫*	sàam saam¹	shān	clothes
袖	jauh jau⁶	xiù	sleeve
被	péih pei⁵	bèi	blacket
袍	pòuh po⁴	páo	gown
裸	ló loh²	luǒ	naked
補	bóu bo²	bǔ	darn, mend
褲	fu foo³	kù	trousers
裙	kwàhn kwan⁴	qún	dress
襪	maht mat⁶	wà	socks, stockings
表	bìu biu¹	biǎo	watch, appearance
袋	doih doi⁶	dài	pocket
女裝	néuih jòng nui⁵ jong¹	nǚ zhuāng	lady's fashion

* 衫 is Cantonese colloquialism, Putonghua speakers use 衣服 .

Activity 1: Write the Chinese Characters.

一 亠 𧘇 𧘇 衣

衣							

ラ 才 衤 衫

衫							

衤 衦 袖 袖

袖							

衤 衫 衬 被

被							

ネ 衤 褚 褲

褲							

ネ 衵 衵 裙

裙							

女　　　丬 爿 壯 裝

女	裝						

亻 代 代 袋

袋							

Activity 2:   Match the Chinese vocabulary with the correct pictures

裙　　　　·　　　　　　·　

袍　　　　·　　　　　　·　

褲　　　　·　　　　　　·　

被　　　　·　　　　　　·　

衫　　　　·　　　　　　·

Unit 19

yìhn   words
yin⁴
yán   speak

The mouth speaks
its lines of words.

例句： 我們在語言中心上課。大家
討論功課。

Example:	We are having lessons in the Language Centre. All of us are discussing the homework.
(Yale)	Ngóh mùhn joih yúh yìhn jùng sàm séuhng fo. Daaih gà tóuh leuhn gùng fo.
(Lau)	Ngoh⁵ moon⁴ joi⁶ yue⁵ yin⁴ jung¹ sam¹ seung⁵ foh. Daai⁶ ga¹ to⁵ leun⁶ gung¹ foh³.
(Pinyin)	Wǒ men zài yǔ yán zhōng xīn shàng kè. Dà jiā tǎo lùn gōng kè.

Radical

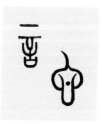

This radical indicates a relationship with words or speech.

	Yale Lau	Pinyin	English
語言	yúh yìhn yue⁵ yin⁴	yǔ yán	language
說	syut suet³	shuō	speak, say (formal)
話 *	wah wa⁶	huà	speak, say (informal)
誰	sèuih sui⁴	shuí	who
認	yihng ying⁶	rèn	admit
請	chéng ching²	qǐng	please
講	góng gong²	jiǎng	speak (colloquial)
課	fo foh³	kè	lesson
課室	fo sàt foh³ sat¹	kè shì	classroom
討論	tóuh leuhn to⁵ leun⁶	tǎo lùn	discuss
功課	gùng fo gung¹ foh³	gōng kè	homework
日記	yaht gei yat⁶ gei³	rì jì	diary
多謝	dò jeh doh¹ je⁶	duō xiè	thank you
讀書	duhk syù duk⁶ sue¹	dú shū	study, read books

* 話 is a colloquial Cantonese meaning "to say." It is also a noun meaning "words."

Activity 1: Write the Chinese Characters.

一 亠 言

言							

言 訂 訂 訝 語　　言

語	言						

言 訥 説

説							

言 訐 話

話							

言 討 討　言 諭 論 論

討	論						

日　言 記 記 記

日	記						

言 訁 訊 課 課

課							

夕 多　言 訉 訷 謝 謝

多	謝						

Activity 2: Match the Chinese vocabulary with the English meaning.

討論 •   • speech

功課 •   • having lesson

課室 •   • discussion

上課 •   • classroom

說話 •   • homework

Activity 3: Circle the vocabulary in the grid. The number in the brackets indicates the number of characters in the word.

多	謝	忘	第	討	論
少	日	記	一	塊	言
小	日	功	課	言	語
請	工	作	室	話	言

please (1)   speak (2)

one piece (2)   language (2)

homework (2)   classroom (2)

lesson 1 (3)   more or less (2)

forget (2)   diary (2)

everyday (2)   work (2)

Unit 20

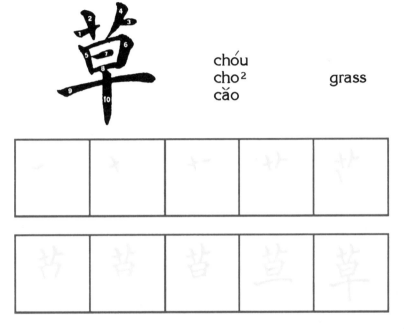

chóu
cho²
cǎo

grass

* For convenience, the radical ⺿ can be written as ⺾ instead, thus resulting in a reduction of one stroke. The stroke order: 一 十 艹

例句： 公園裏，花草多，落葉也多。

Example: In the park, (there are) lots of flowers and grass. Falling leaves are also plentiful.

(Yale) Gùng yùn léuih, fà chóu dò, lohk yihp yáh dò.

(Lau) Gung¹ yuen⁴ lui⁵, fa¹ cho² doh¹, lok⁶ yip⁶ ya⁵ doh¹.

(Pinyin) Gōng yuán lǐ, huā cǎo duō, luò yè yě dūo.

Radical

This radical indicates a relationship with plants.

109

	Yale Lau	Pinyin	English
花	fà fa¹	huā	*flower*
草	chóu cho²	cǎo	*grass*
茶	chàh cha⁴	chá	*tea*
菜	choi choi³	cài	*vegetable*
苦	fú foo²	kǔ	*bitter*
葱	chùng chung¹	cōng	*spring onion*
葉	yihp yip⁶	yè	*leaves*
薯	syúh su⁵	shǔ	*potato*
落	lohk lok⁶	luò	*going down*
薑	gèung gueng¹	jiāng	*ginger*
菠菜	bò choi boh¹ choi³	bō cài	*spinach*
落葉	lohk yihp lok⁶ yip⁶	luò yè	*falling leaves*
香蕉	hēung jìu heung¹ jiu¹	xiāng jiāo	*banana*
蘋果	pìhng gwó ping⁴ gwoh²	pín guǒ	*apple*

Activity 1:   Write the Chinese Characters.

⺾ 艹 花 花

花							

⺾ 苩 草

草							

⺾ 犬 茶

茶							

⺾ 꿈 菜

菜							

艹 芢 苦

苦 | | | | | | |

艹 芐 茨 落

落 | | | | | | |

艹 芏 芊 芅 葉

葉 | | | | | | |

艹 芢 苼 莊 萑 蕉

蕉 | | | | | | |

Activity 2:   Match the Chinese vocabulary with the pictures.

菜   ·   ·

花   ·   ·

草   ·   ·

茶   ·   ·

葉   ·   ·

Unit 21 Revision Exercises

(I) **Multiple Choice: Circle the suitable Chinese character to complete the sentence.**

1. 我們（吃，哈，唱）歌。
2. 她時常吃（橙，燈，汽）。
3. 他想要一（檯，根，杯）橙汁。
4. 我去洗手間（游，河，洗）手。
5. 李太太的子女在家裏討論
   功（課，語，記）。
6. 她（姊，姓，婚）李。
7. 我們是（好，大，女）朋友。
8. 星期日我們去（海，洗，游）水。
9. 我（拉，推，坐）小巴上學。
10. 她哈哈大（話，笑，語）。

(II) **Who is saying what?**
Write the suitable Chinese characters in the bubbles to match the picture. You can choose the characters from the box below.

1.

_____

2.

_____

3.

_____

4.

_____

5.

_____

6.

_____

小心！　很熱！　奇怪！
好吃！　請喝茶。　來！

(III) Write the missing radicals to complete the Chinese characters.

1.

七　寺

2.

兑　舌

3.

田　相

4.

化　早

5.

先　面

6.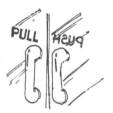

隹　立

(IV) Write the Chinese character which has the opposite meaning to the English one. You can choose the Chinese characters from the box below.

1. stand ↔
2. late ↔
3. cry ↔
4. clever ↔
5. sweet ↔
6. going up ↔
7. slow ↔
8. bad ↔
9. blunt ↔

落快笨早好坐尖笑苦

(V) Which picture corresponds to the sentence?
Circle the number of the picture.

1. 明天是五月三日。

A   B   C

2. 課室裏不准吸煙。

A   B   C

3. 檯上有香蕉和蘋果。

A   B   C

4. 語言中心今天休息。

A   B   C

5. 媽媽買了裙和褲。

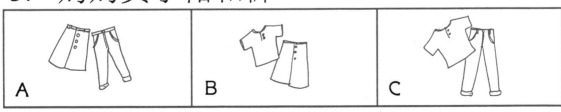

A   B   C

True or False?
Study the picture below and then decide whether the sentences are true or false.

1. 檯上有一杯果汁。 　　　　　　　（　　）

2. 地下有一箱橙。 　　　　　　　　（　　）

3. 今天天氣很炎熱。 　　　　　　　（　　）

4. 一個女孩子在看電視。 　　　　　（　　）

5. 今天是四月五日星期六。 　　　　（　　）

6. 家裏有很多人。 　　　　　　　　（　　）

7. 一個男孩子在看書。 　　　　　　（　　）

(VII) Spot the mistakes:
Each sentence below contains one character used wrongly. Identify and underline the mistake and write the correct answer in the brackets. The first one is done for you.

1. 妹妹在樹上<u>倡</u>歌。 （ 唱 ）

2. 媽媽昨天抄菠菜。 （　　）

3. 我很口渴，我想渴水。 （　　）

4. 李太太用分切橙時很小心。 （　　）

5. 姊姊在可裏游水。 （　　）

6. 課室裏不准吸溫。 （　　）

(VIII) Fill in the blanks with suitable Chinese characters to complete the sentences. You can choose the characters from the box below.

1. 他們是（　　　）朋友。

2. 樹上有很多樹（　　　）。

3. 我媽媽的媽媽是我
　的（　　）（　　）。

4. 我用（　　　）看書，
　用口（　　　）點心。

5. 星（　　　）日我們去游水。

6. 小心！這把刀很（　　　）。

Answers

Unit 1

Activity 3: 1.今   2.你們   3.住   4.信   5.傘   6.休

Unit 2

Activity 3: 1.剪刀 2.切   3.分   4.別

Unit 3

Activity 2: 1.吹   2.唱   3.吻   4.問   5.哈   6.叫

Activity 3: 1.吻   2.哈   3.吃   4.問   5.唱

Unit 4

Activity 3: 1.一堆   2.壞   3.地   4.坐

Unit 5

Activity 3:   1.火車裏很炎熱。
2.大家很奇怪。
3.他天天在大學吃飯。
4.今天大家休息。

Unit 6

Activity 2: 1.少   2.多   3.大   4.小   5.尖   6.小心

7.小姐   8.小學

Unit 8

Activity 3: 1.孫   2.字   3.孩   4.學   5. 仔   6.孕

Unit 9

Activity 2: a.想   b.恨   c.忙   d.快, 點心   e.必要, 中心
f. 好, 怪

Unit 10

Activity 2: 1.手表　2.洗手　3.手指　4.拉　5.捉　6.推

Unit 11

Activity 3: 1.是　2.明日（天）3.昨日（天）是
4.小時　5.星期

Unit 12

Activity 3: 1.我明天吃月餅。（明天我吃月餅。）
2.她是我的好朋友。
3.昨日天氣晴朗。
4.三月有三十一日。

Unit 13

Activity 2: 1.杯　2.根　3.橙　4.樹　5.村　6.梨

Unit 14

Activity 2: 1.e 2.f 3.a 4.c 5.d 6.b
Activity 3: 1.汗　2.汽　3.湯　4.洗　5.深　6.汁

Unit 16

Activity 3: 1.眼　2.睡　3.相　4.看　5.盲　6.直

Unit 17

Activity 2: 1.笑　2.簿　3.筆　4.箱　5.第三　6.計算

Unit 21

I:　1.唱　2.橙　3.杯　4.洗　5.課
6.姓　7.好　8.游　9.坐　10.笑

II: 1.很熱！　2.奇怪！　3.小心！4.請喝茶。5.來！
6.好吃！

III: 1.時　2.説話　3.思想　4.花草　5.洗面　6.推拉

IV: 1.坐　2.早　3.笑　4.笨　5.苦　6.落　7.快　8.好　9.尖

V: 　1. B 　2. A 　3. C 　4. C 　5. A

VI: 　1. T 　2. T 　3.T 　4. F 　5. T 　6. F 　7. T

VII: 　2.抄→炒 　3.渴→喝（水） 　4.分→刀 　5. 可→河
　　6.湮→煙

VII: 　1.好 　2.葉 　3.婆婆 　4.眼,吃 　5.期 　6.尖／利

Index

味	咬	哈	唱	問
taste	bite	ha ha	sing	ask

喝
drink

29

土
land

地	地	址	坐	城
ground	address		sit	city
埋	基	堂	堆	堅
bury	base	hall	heap	strong
場	塊	填	壞	塵
venue	piece	fill	broken	dust

34

大
big

太	天	奇	獎
too / Mrs	day / sky	strange	prize

39

小
small

少	尖
less	sharp

44 女 girl	奶 milk	她 she	好 good	姊 elder sister	妹 younger sis
	妻 wife	姓 surname	姑 aunt	姦 rape	婆 grandmom
	媽 mother				

49 子 son	字 word	孕 pregnant	孩 child	孫 grandchild	學 learn

54 心 heart	必 must	忙 busy	快 quick	忘 forget	怪 weird
	思 think of	急 urgent	恨 hate	息 rest	想 think
	恐 怕 afraid				

59	手 hand	打 hit	抄 copy	折 break	拉 pull	抱 hold
		指 point/finger	捉 catch	推 push	掌 palm	

64	日 sun	早 early	昌 prosperous	明 bright	星 star	昨 yesterday
		是 is, am, are	春 spring	時 hour/time	晚 evening	晨 morning
		晶 shinny	晴 sunny			

69	月 moon	有 have	朋 friend	服 clothes	朗 sunny	期 date

74	木 wood	本 base	材 timber	村 village	林 forest	杯 cup

果	桃	根	梨	森
fruit	peach	root	pear	jungle
橙	樹	橋	檯	
orange	tree	bridge	table	

79 水 water

汁	池	汗	汽	水
juice	pool	sweat	soft drink	
河	泳	洗	洋	海
river	swim	wash	ocean	sea
淚	淺	深	游	湯
tear	shallow	deep	swim	soup

84 火 fire

炒	炎	炭	煙	煩
fry	very hot	coal	smoke	trouble
煮	煲	熱	燈	熟
cook	boil/pot	hot	lamp	cooked

燒				
burn				

89

目	盲	直	眉	相	省
eye	blind	straight	eyebrow	photo	province
	看	真	眾	眼	睇
	look	real	crowd	eye	watch
	睡				
	sleep				

94

竹	笑	笨	第	等	筆
bamboo	laugh	stupid	numerical	wait/class	pen
	答	算	箱	簽	簿
	answer	calculate	box	sign	book
	籃	籠			
	basket	cage			

99 衣 clothes	表 watch	衫 clothes	袖 sleeve	被 blanket	袍 gown
	袋 pocket	裙 dress	補 darn, mend	裝 fashion	裸 naked
	褲 trousers	襪 socks			

104 言 speech	討 discuss	論	記 remember	話 say/words	説 speak
	語 language	認 admit	課 lesson	請 please	誰 who
	謝 thank	講 speak	讀 read		

109 草 grass	花 flower	苦 bitter	茶 tea	菜 vegetable	菠 spinach

落	葉	葱	蕉	薯
falling	leaf	spring onion	banana	potato

薑	蘋
ginger	apple

Appendix - Simplified Chinese Characters

The written forms of Cantonese and Mainland Chinese share many of the same characters. Mainland China, however, uses some characters which are simpler to read and write than the 'traditional' forms used in Hong Kong, Taiwan and much of the rest of Asia.

The following chart gives a list of those characters used in this book that have 'simplified' forms. The left hand side of each column presents the characters as they have been used in the book while their 'simplified' equivalents are shown on the right:

來	↔	来	媽	↔	妈
們	↔	们	孫	↔	孙
傘	↔	伞	學	↔	学
劍	↔	剑	時	↔	时
問	↔	问	樹	↔	树
堅	↔	坚	橋	↔	桥
場	↔	场	檯	↔	枱
塊	↔	块	淺	↔	浅
壞	↔	坏	湯	↔	汤
塵	↔	尘	煩	↔	烦
獎	↔	奖	熱	↔	热

燈	↔	灯		課	↔	课
燒	↔	烧		請	↔	请
筆	↔	笔		誰	↔	谁
籤	↔	签		謝	↔	谢
籃	↔	篮		講	↔	讲
籠	↔	笼		讀	↔	读
補	↔	补		葉	↔	叶
裝	↔	装		蘋	↔	萍
褲	↔	裤				
襪	↔	袜				
討	↔	讨				
論	↔	论				
記	↔	记				
話	↔	话				
説	↔	说				
語	↔	语				
認	↔	认				